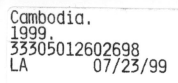

FIESTA!

CAMBODIA

GROLIER
EDUCATIONAL

Published 1999 by Grolier Educational
Sherman Turnpike, Danbury, Connecticut.
Copyright © 1999 Times Editions Pte Ltd. Singapore.

Set ISBN: 0-7172-9324-6
Volume ISBN: 0-7172-9326-2

CIP information available from the Library of Congress or the publisher

Brown Partworks Ltd.

Series Editor: Tessa Paul
Series Designer: Joyce Mason
Crafts devised and created by Susan Moxley
Music arrangements by Harry Boteler
Photographs by Bruce Mackie
Subeditor: Annette Cheyne
Production: Alex Mackenzie
Stylists: Joyce Mason and Tessa Paul

For this volume:
Designer: Joan Curtis
Writer: Paul Thompson
Consultant: Sayron Lao
Editorial Assistants: Hannah Beardon and Paul Thompson

Printed in Italy

Adult supervision advised for all crafts and recipes,
particularly those involving sharp instruments and heat.

CONTENTS

CAMBODIA:

Cambodia is part of Southeast Asia and lies on the Indochinese Peninsula. Its main river is the Mekong, which keeps the land fertile.

Thailand

Myanmar

Andaman Sea

▶ **The Mekong River** is vital to life in Cambodia. People depend on it for fish and rice. The river floods every year, making the land fertile and naturally irrigating the rice paddies.

First Impressions

- **Population** 9,968,000
- **Largest city** Phnom Penh with a population of 700,000
- **Longest river** Mekong
- **Highest mountains** Cardamom Mts. up to 5,948 ft.
- **Exports** Rubber, rice, cattle
- **Capital city** Phnom Penh
- **Political status** Constitutional monarchy
- **Climate** Tropical climate, with heavy seasonal rain called monsoon
- **Art and culture** Famous for its beautiful silks, graceful traditional dances, and its many Buddhist temples.

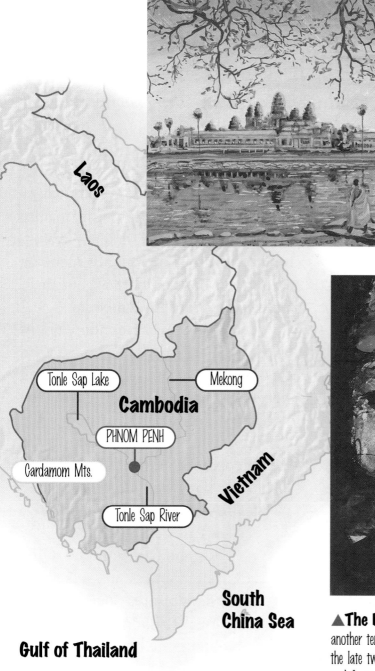

◀ **Angkor Wat** contains more than 100 temples that were built between the seventh and the eleventh centuries. They are part of a spectacular center built by the mighty Khmer god-kings. From here they ruled a vast empire that stretched from the tip of southern Vietnam to China.

Laos

Tonle Sap Lake — Mekong

Cambodia

PHNOM PENH

Cardamom Mts.

Tonle Sap River

Vietnam

South China Sea

Gulf of Thailand

▲**The Bayon**, to the north of Angkor Wat, is another temple built by the Khmers and dates from the late twelfth century. The buildings are very ornate and fantastic to look at. The temple contains over 200 giant carved faces and is also famous for its bas-reliefs, carvings that tell in stone the history of the Khmer god-kings.

RELIGIONS

Most Cambodians follow a kind of Buddhism called **Theravada Buddhism,** *which means "The Way of the Elders." Buddhism is the most common religion in Cambodia, but Islam and Christianity are also practiced.*

AN OLD FORM of Buddhism that looks only to the writings of the early Buddhists, *Theravada Buddhism* was first practiced in Cambodia in the thirteenth or fourteenth century. Buddhists believe that a young prince called Siddhartha gave up his life of luxury to find enlightenment. It took him many years to find this and, when he did, he was called Buddha, meaning "enlightened one."

When the teachings of Buddha were brought to Cambodia, the royal family believed in Hinduism. This religion came from India. Its followers worship many gods. A Cambodian king, Suryavarman II, built an amazing temple to the Hindu god Vishnu. The ruins of this temple, Angkor Wat, can still be seen. Buddhism mixed with the teachings of Hinduism spread across Cambodia to become the national religion.

The Islamic faith arrived in Southeast Asia with Arab traders in the thirteenth century, but only a small number of Cambodians adopted this new religion. Christianity was introduced to the country mainly by the French who brought Cambodia under their control in 1864, but there are few Christians in Cambodia.

Cambodia became independent from France in 1953. Since then the country has suffered a long civil war as the people within the country fight each other. One group, the Khmer Rouge, controlled the country from 1975 to 1979. They banned religion and destroyed many holy buildings and statues.

Cambodians are now trying to make their country a peaceful one. Buddhism is once more the national religion, and the holy buildings are being restored.

This pillar is part of the Royal Palace's pavilion. The four faces of Buddha align with the cardinal points of the world.

GREETINGS FROM **CAMBODIA!**

About nine million people speak Khmer, or the Cambodian language. It is one of the oldest languages of Southeast Asia. Khmer texts carved in stone have been found. They are over a thousand years old. Modern Khmer uses many French words as Cambodia was part of the French colony of Indo-China for almost a century. In the remote hill regions and jungles the people speak dialects of Khmer. A dialect is a version of the main language.

Cambodia is about the same size as the state of Missouri. There are a number of lakes, and a mighty river, the Mekong, runs through the country. Where it runs into the sea it forms a delta. This means the river breaks into many smaller rivers, and the land between these streams is rich and fertile. Cambodians build their houses on stilts so that they stay dry, no matter how high the river or the lakes rise. Most people are farmers. They grow rice in the wet delta and have fish farms. Inland there are dense jungles and high mountain ranges. The farmers have to move every few years, looking for new, more fertile land on which to grow food.

How do you say...

Hello
Johm riab sua

How are you?
Niak sohk sabbay te?

My name is...
Kh'nyohm ch'muah...

Goodbye
Lia suhn hao-y

Thank you
Aw kohn

Peace
Sontepeap

COL CHNAM THMEI

*The Cambodian New Year is a time for renewal and celebration. Everyone welcomes the new **devada**, or "angels," who will bless them with prosperity, happiness, and luck.*

The Cambodians celebrate two New Years. One is for the beginning of the solar year, while one is for the beginning of the lunar year. The chief celebration is for the Solar New Year. This begins, according to our Western calendar, on April 13. The festivities last for three days, and they are marked

TEMPLE MUSIC

Groups of musicians form small orchestras. They play traditional percussion instruments, including the circular percussion, different types of drums, and a xylophone. The music often accompanies dance performances or religious rituals.

by religious rituals and dances. This is also a time when families visit each other.

The first day of the New Year is particularly special. From the Royal Palace comes the sound of conch shells, which make a noise like that of trumpets. The conch shell musicians blow three notes. This is a sign for the king to show himself to his people before going to an altar in his palace.

Cambodians do not send their prayers only to the Buddha. They believe that there are

Burning incense sticks and coils is an important part of many religious rituals all over the world. In Cambodia it is a part of worship on the day of New Year.

COL CHNAM THMEI

Or kah col chnam pra cam ceat _____ Noamang knear

sang saat a laing ka _____ Bo cear

bang koom de pada Som se rei cei __ so - ka

Cenda ponn pang _____

Enjoying traditional food is a special part of the New Year festivities. Fish wrapped in cabbage is a popular festive dish in Cambodia.

other deities around him, and they give praise and offerings to these lesser gods.

On this first day of the Solar New Year the king prays to these deities. They are believed to protect not only his country but the rest of the world too. When the king finishes, a priest prays for the health and happiness of the entire nation. He asks for peace and abundance in the land. The king prays once more, and musicians blow the conch shells three more times to end the ritual.

Groups of musicians form orchestras, and female dancers perform religious dances. All the movements are meaningful and often relate to the Buddha or the deities who surround the Buddha.

All over the country people worship on the day of the Solar New Year. The numerous temples, called *wats*, are full of people. Even the huge and magnificent Angkor Wat, a ruined temple, becomes a place of worship at this time.

People also set up altars in front of their homes. Incense sticks are burned, and the altars are decorated with displays of flowers, fruit, and drinks. These are offerings to the *devada*, or "angels." The worshippers hope that, in exchange for the offerings, they will receive the blessings of the devada.

For the New Year Cambodians construct tall cones of sand. They

This statue shows the supreme god Vishnu sitting on a snake. Serpent deities are often worshipped as companions of the gods.

ANGKOR WAT

The ruined temple of Angkor Wat in northwest Cambodia was built in the twelfth century by King Suryavarman II. The Hindu temple is one of the architectural wonders of the ancient Khmer Empire.

The temple was "discovered" by a French explorer, Henri Mouhot, on one of his voyages of exploration (1858–1860). But long before him some Portuguese travelers had found the site, and a Japanese pilgrim had even drawn plans of the temple.

decorate these with incense sticks, candles, and strips of brightly colored fabric. People say prayers for the dead; as they do so, they hold onto the fabric strips. The mounds of sand symbolize the points of the compass. There is a mountain at the center of the world, and one at each point, north, south, east, and west, of the compass.

New Year is also a popular time for games.

The most exciting is a tug of war between men and women. They use a rope made of rattan. The men and women struggle to pull against their opponents, while the crowds shout for the team they support.

Another game often played at New Year is *sey*. This game is played by men and boys. They stand in a circle in two teams. The sey, a small feathered object, can be hit by any part of the body except the hands. Both teams try to keep the sey in the air, and they lose points if it falls to the ground.

The devada have not been kind over the last 40 years. Perhaps, now that peace has come, the angels will bless Cambodia and its hopeful people.

The celebration of New Year is also a time of merry making. One popular game involves passing this feathered object, the sey, to each other without it touching the ground.

CHURNING THE SEA OF MILK

This creation story comes from the Hindu religion but is also popular in Buddhism. The temple of Angkor Wat is decorated with many sculptures illustrating the story.

LONG AGO THE SEAS had risen and flooded the land. All the precious treasures of the gods were lost in this great flood. Among these was the elixir of immortality called Soma. The minor gods had to find this elixir because without it they would not live forever. Even the great gods such as Shiva and Vishnu needed it to give them strength.

The elixir made the sea look milky. The gods guessed that they could retrieve the Soma if they churned the sea as they would churn milk. Perhaps the

Soma would separate from it as butter separates from milk. Without the Soma the gods felt weak so they needed the demons to help them with the churning.

They promised the demons some of the Soma if they helped. The gods were lying – they had no intention of making the demons more powerful by letting them drink the Soma.

To churn the sea a churning pole was needed. A mountain that rested on the bottom of the ocean was used for this. The huge, many-headed Naga serpent

wrapped itself like a rope around the mountain. The demons pulled on one side and the gods on the other. As they pulled the churning pole with the Naga, the pole began to move.

Vishnu became worried. He saw that the churning of the milky sea was causing the earth to tremble. He realized that the earth would crumble into

pieces so he changed himself into a huge tortoise and rested the churning pole on his back. This immediately calmed the movement of the earth.

Slowly the lost treasures began to emerge from the milk. One of these was a beautiful goddess called Lakshmi. She became the wife of Vishnu. A terrible poison also came out of the milk. It was so strong that it was able to harm all the gods, but Shiva swallowed the poison and kept it safely in his throat.

Gradually the Soma emerged. The gods and the demons began to fight for it. The demons managed to run off with it, but Vishnu came to the rescue again. He turned himself into a beautiful woman called Mohini. She was so beautiful that the demons were bewitched. They gave her the Soma, and she passed it to the gods.

VISAKH BOCHEA

One month during the full moon there are two celebrations— the Salakaphot *and* Visakh Bochea.

To recall the birth, enlightenment, and death of the Buddha, people light candles and burn incense.

Two very important celebrations take place during the month of Visakh. The Salakaphot is an offering to the Buddhist priests, while Visakh Bochea honors the life of Buddha.

On the day of Visakh Bochea all the pagodas of Cambodia are lit up with candles that burn all day and all night, and the air is fragrant with the smell of incense. During this time the faithful sit in the temple listening to the monks read from the holy Buddhist texts. At the same time a similar private ritual takes place in the palace for the royal family.

The whole day is dedicated to the birth of the Buddha. The faithful also use his birthday to remember his enlightenment and his death. It is a quiet

Ornate carvings and lavish temple decorations contrast with the simple life of the monks in the monasteries.

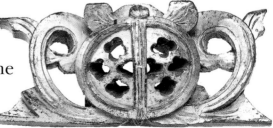

and solemn day when believers take time to think deeply about Buddha's teachings.

The Salakaphot is a ceremonial gift of fruit and flowers to the monks. These are the holy men of Buddhism. They live

Bells are used to mark religious activities and call the faithful to worship. In many eastern cultures they are also associated with magic and ritual.

simple lives and do not strive for money or possessions. Most Cambodian boys will spend some time in a temple, living as

BUDDHISM

Buddha was born around 560 B.C. He was the son of a king and was called Siddhartha Gautama. He grew up in a life of luxury in his father's palace. When he was a young man, he saw the poverty and suffering that mark most people's lives. He immediately decided to give up luxury and to devote his life to the search for wisdom.

Buddhism centers upon the truth that all human beings suffer, and then asks how they may be released from suffering. The teachings of the Buddha show how to achieve this — by doing good, by not hurting others, and by overcoming greed. Buddhists also meditate to find peace and release from suffering. "To meditate" means to sit quietly and have spiritual thoughts.

monks, so they learn to appreciate the monks' humble life. This taking of offerings to the temples emphasizes the respect people feel for monks.

The ceremony of the Salakaphot starts with pieces of paper, each bearing the name of a monk, being placed in a bowl. The faithful each draw one piece of paper and give food to the monk whose name is on the paper. At the palace the king uses a gold bowl that holds a single piece of paper bearing the name of the chief monk.

15

BONN CHRAT PREAH NONGKOAL

The traditional Royal Plowing Festival is very important – the king himself attends the festival. In Cambodia many people still farm the land and grow their own food.

The *Bonn Chrat Preah Nongkoal* ceremony, or the Royal Plowing Festival, is related to beliefs that go back over 1,000 years. The ritual is also very old. Early civilizations did not understand the science of farming. People danced, sang, or made offerings of food to bring good weather and soil to grow good crops.

Some of these old ideas are revealed in the traditional Royal Plowing Festival. The field where the ritual takes place is called the Veal Mean. It is in front of the Royal Palace in the capital city, Phnom Penh. The land set aside

For centuries buffaloes have been tamed for domestic use and are easily handled, even by children. The statue on the left shows the elephant-headed god Ganesha, the son of Shiva.

for the ritual is surrounded by five pavilions. Of these, four hold a statue of a Hindu god. In the first there is Shiva;

another has Brahma, and the other two have Vishnu and Ganesha. The fifth contains a statue of Preah Kampchay, who was a disciple of Buddha.

In front of each pavilion is a mound of earth with the top hollowed out. The mounds are covered with cloth and sheltered by parasols. In each of the hollows burns a fire. As the fire is lit, the monks read verses. Conch shells sound three times. This is the signal for the water buffaloes to start pulling the sacred plows around the field. Water buffaloes are important in the lives of Cambodian farmers. They haul the plows, provide

This bronze statuette shows the dancing figure of the Hindu god Shiva. The four arms symbolize his endless activities.

milk and carry heavy burdens.

There are three plows in the Bonn Chrat Preah Nongkoal ceremony. The one in the middle is beautifully decorated with bells, flowers, and ribbons. This is the "noble plow." It is steered by the "King of Meakh" who is played by the king of Cambodia. If the king is not available, one of his ministers plays this role. As the King of Meakh steers the noble plow, he is followed

Pretty painted parasols shelter the mounds of earth.

The Cambodian bank note on the right illustrates the plowing ceremony.

The buffaloes eat from large silver dishes. This dish shows common Cambodian animals. According to local belief each animal represents a different year or season.

by the "Queen Me Hour." Usually the real queen of Cambodia plays this part. She walks behind the plow, scattering rice seeds. The rice must be of the very best quality.

The other two plows are steered by civil servants. The plows make three turns, and the conch shells trumpet at each turn.

The plows stop in front of the east pavil-ion, which contains the statue of Vishnu. This god is worshipped as the protector of the world and the restorer of moral order.

At the east pavilion the three buffaloes are unharnessed, and the leader of the monks prays to the gods, ask-ing them to let the forthcoming season be good for the crops. The priest then uses clean, pure water to bless the buffalo that was harnessed to the noble plow. At this point everybody in the

Lemon grass is offered to the buffaloes during the ceremony.

The fabric shows images of chickens, horses, and temples.

crowd feels tense and excited. This is because the royal astrologer is preparing to read the omens, and the crowd is anxious to hear whether there will be a bumper crop or a poor season in the next growing year.

The water buffaloes are led to seven large silver plates, each of which contains differ-ent kinds of foods and drinks. There are bowls of rice, beans, wine, and grass. The royal

EXOTIC FRUIT SALAD

Place the orange juice, lime juice, and sugar in a large glass mixing bowl. Stir this mixture until the sugar dissolves.
Carefully open the canned fruit. Place a sieve over a small bowl and pour the canned fruit into the sieve. Add 1–2 T. of canned-fruit liquid to the juice mixture — stir again. Add the canned fruit.
Ask an adult to cut the honeydew melon in half. Remove and then discard the seeds with a large metal spoon. Use a melon baller to scoop out the melon flesh into small balls. Add the melon balls to the other fruit. Stir gently until everything is well mixed.
You can serve this right away — but fruit salad tastes even better if you chill it in the refrigerator for an hour or more.

SERVES 4
¼ cup orange juice
1 T. lime juice
2 t. sugar
One 15-oz can lychees
One 11-oz can mandarin oranges
1 honeydew melon

astrologer, a highly respected man in the palace, becomes the center of the crowd's attention. He knows how to read the stars, and people believe he can predict future events. He watches closely to see what the buffaloes eat and drink. He believes their choice shows how the season will develop. For example, if the buffaloes drink from a bowl containing water, then according to the old beliefs there will be a lot of rain in the coming year. If they eat the grain, the harvest will be bountiful.

BUDDHA AND THE JAMBU TREE

This delightful tale is about Buddha as a small child. It confirms that even when he was a young boy, he showed all the signs of becoming a great spiritual leader.

ONE DAY WHEN the Buddha was only a baby, he was taken by his nurses for a day out to the state plowing festival. It was a lovely sunny day so the nurses left little Siddhartha sleeping in the cool, protective shade of a jambu tree.

The nurses began to watch the ceremony in which the king, his ministers, and the farmers all took part. The colorful scene was so fascinating that they forgot about the sleeping Siddhartha and left him by the tree as they moved to take a closer look at the ceremony.

They stood together among the crowds watching the plows being pulled by strong buffaloes. They saw the king, Siddhartha's father, looking on at the spectacle in his fine clothes.

The nurses were enjoying the festivities so much that they did not remember the sleeping child for hours. Ashamed that they had forgotten the little prince, they hurried back to the jambu tree. Now they were extremely worried that some harm might have come to him in their absence.

When they reached the tree, they immediately noticed that the sun had

moved across the sky, but the tree's dark shadow had not moved at all. This big shadow had stayed in the exact same place in order to protect the tiny child who would in the future be the Buddha.

The nurses were astonished to find that he was sitting upright with his legs crossed. He was absorbed in meditation just like a grown-up monk. The nurses called for his father, who was also amazed to see his son in this pose.

The king recalled that when the child was born, the highest priests in the land had come to see him. Eight of these priests had been experts in reading the marks on a baby's body. Seven of them had said his son was sure to grow up to be a great king or a Buddha. The eighth and youngest priest had been certain that he would definitely be a Buddha. Looking at his child, the king remembered what the priests had said. He knelt down and worshipped his baby son.

Another tree was to play an important part in the prince's life. One day, as a young man, he sat beneath a fig tree. He said he would not move until he became enlightened. He meditated under the tree for 49 days, and finally he reached a state of peace called *nirvana*. From this day on he held the title "Buddha."

KAN BEN

In this 15-day festival Cambodians remember the souls of their ancestors. Buddhists show respect for the dead by giving gifts to their ancestors.

On the first day of *Kan Ben*, Yama the king of the underworld sets free the souls of the dead so that they can mingle with the living. It is said that if the souls visit seven pagodas and do not find any offerings, they will curse their families.

The word *ben* refers to temple offerings. They are bowls of rice cooked in coconut milk. They are arranged around a larger, central bowl of rice. The rice inside the central bowl is shaped into a cone that is covered with banana leaves. Candles, flowers, and incense sticks are put on top.

On each festival day people place a bowl of

Originally pagodas were shrines for housing the relics of Buddha. The dead are believed to visit seven pagodas in their search for offerings.

BANANAS COOKED IN COCONUT MILK

Carefully open the can of coconut milk and pour it into a medium saucepan. Add the sugar to the saucepan. Now place this mixture over a fairly high heat and bring it to a boil — stir once or twice with a wooden spoon. Once it boils, lower the heat until the mixture is gently bubbling. Continue to cook until it is thick and creamy, stirring now and then.

While the milk cooks, peel the bananas and cut them into large pieces. Stir them into the coconut milk and cook for five minutes, until they are hot but not mushy.

Serve warm.

SERVES 6
2 cups canned coconut milk
2 T. sugar or brown sugar
6 large ripe bananas

rice around the central cone so that on the last day there are 15 bowls of rice around the central bowl.

Another important offering made at this time is called *Phkar Ben*. It is a flower offering in the shape of a pyramid. It is made from brightly colored paper flowers on a stick of bamboo. On top of this arrangement is a figure of a mythical bird holding a candle.

On the evening of the last day of Kan Ben families hold a big dinner to honor the dead. The head of the family lights candles to invite the dead to join the festivities. The dead are asked to watch over the whole family.

During the festival of Kan Ben the whole country is on the move, and traffic jams are a common sight in the cities. In poor rural areas the traditional form of transport – carts pulled by oxen – can still be seen on country roads.

MAKE A PAPER KITE

Toward the end of November children all over Cambodia can be seen flying brightly colored kites.

Kite flying is all that remains of an ancient full moon festival. The king and the priests used to fly the kites in the fall. They flew them at night with small lamps attached to them so that they glowed against the night sky. Not much else is known about this festival, but kite flying is still very popular in Cambodia. Make two Cambodian kites to fly on a windy day.

A

B

YOU WILL NEED
Colored Japanese paper
Colored tissue paper
Wooden skewer sticks
All-purpose glue
Needle
Thread
Paints
Scissors
Pencil

1 Cut out a snake head (A) from Japanese paper and a tissue-paper tail. Draw and color head (B). Cut one skewer to fit length of head and one to fit width. Glue to back of head in a cross. Glue tail to head. Add threads and handle — see step three.

2 Cut a star from Japanese paper and two long, thin tails from tissue paper. Also cut small tissue diamonds. Cut one skewer to fit the length of star, one to fit across it, and two to fit diagonally (C). Glue them to the back of star. Glue the diamonds and tails in place.

3 Stitch a 15" piece of thread through top of star around skewer (D); knot the end. Tie an 8" piece of thread to the first piece (about halfway down) and stitch the other end around skewer (E). Tie the end of 15" thread to a separate skewer — use this stick as a handle to pull the kite. Follow the same method to attach threads and handle for snake kite.

25

BON OM TUK

The Water Festival celebrates the end of the rainy season. Throughout the rainy season the Mekong River, its streams, and its lakes overflow the land and paddy fields.

Fish forms a major part of the local diet.

In Cambodia the end of the rainy season is celebrated in many different ways. People give gifts of new orange robes to the monks in the monasteries. Picnics are held at which people eat fish and turtles. The most popular event, however, is *Bon Om Tuk*, or the Water Festival which is held to give thanks to the spirit of the water.

People travel from miles away to watch the three days of boat races. They line the banks of the Tonle Sap River, which flows through the capital of Phnom Penh. Everyone cheers for the boat that represents their town. Boats from the 22 provinces of Cambodia come to

Conch shells and other instruments make up the band that plays for the king and his family.

MUSIC AND DANCE

Cambodian music and dance contain elements from a mixture of cultures including Thai, Indian, and Javanese. Traditionally the music is part of a religious performance, often held before the king. The dancers are dressed in brightly colored, sequined costumes. They use expressive hand movements and often act out a religious story to the sound of haunting music played on percussion instruments, flutes, and sometimes a fiddle.

the annual festival. Some get there by road, others travel by river. Each boat has about 30 to 40 rowers. The rowers are brightly dressed and the boats finely decorated. There are two types of boats. In the *Tuk Ngor* boats rowers sit down; on the *Tuk Muong* boats the rowers have to stand during the race!

The first day of the festival begins with the king giving offerings to the royal family in the Silver Pagoda. He then visits altars in front of the palace. These altars are dedicated to different spirits.

On the second day of the boat races offerings and prayers are made. Dances are performed in front of the king and the royal family.

During the third and last day of the Water Festival there is a ceremony called "Prayers to the Full Moon." This ceremony is held to predict the rains in the year ahead. People give offerings of food to the moon, and a special priest called an *achar* prays to the spirits. The achar has the ability to foretell the future.

MAKE A PAPER HOUSEBOAT

Floating houses are made at the end of the Water Festival. Their candles light up the evening waters of the Mekong River.

Each floating house is paid for by a town or company. There is much rivalry to see who can create the most beautiful example. Make your own houseboat and raft — but it is not made to float. Never light candles without an adult's help.

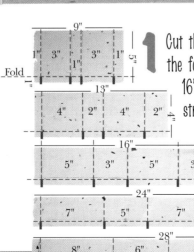

YOU WILL NEED

Pencil and ruler
Handmade or Japanese paper
Scissors
Pinking shears
Different colored paper
All-purpose glue
Skewer sticks
Wooden bamboo sticks
Raffia
Birthday candles
Sticky putty

1 Cut the handmade paper into five strips to the following dimensions: 9" x 5", 13" x 4", 16" x 4", 24" x 3", and 28" x 2". Mark the strips as shown, then fold on the dotted lines. Now make 1" cuts up from the bottom — indicated by the **bold** blue lines. With pinking shears cut along the very top edge of each strip.

Fold

9" 1" 3" 3" 1" 5"
    1"

13" 4" 2" 4" 2" 4"

16" 5" 3" 5" 3" 4"

24" 7" 5" 7" 5" 3"

28" 8" 6" 8" 6" 2"

2 Cut doors from the colored paper and glue onto strips. Fold into rectangular boxes (right) and glue the 1" side flap. Fold bottom flaps in, but do not glue.

3 Find a piece of paper that fits the biggest box. Center the smallest box on the paper and use the bottom flaps to glue it down firmly. Glue the other boxes around it in the same manner.

4 Cut out triangular flag shapes from the colored paper. Glue the flags onto the skewer sticks and glue into the corners of the boxes.

5 For the raft ask an adult to cut bamboo into 14 (13") sticks. To bind them together, wrap the raffia around the first stick, knot it, and wrap it again. Then wrap it around the second stick, knot it, and wrap it again. Continue until all sticks are tied. Do the other side.

6 Glue the houseboat to the raft and surround with birthday candles attached with sticky putty. Ask an adult to help you light the candles.

THE KING'S BIRTHDAY

The civil war did not drive the royal family away forever. In 1993 King Sihanouk was reinstated as king. His birthday festivities last five days.

The rituals surrounding the king's birthday are meant to help him live a long life. On the evening of the first day of the celebrations the king lights a candle, the "Candle of Victory," in the throne room.

This candle burns for three days, and the king can't leave the palace. A group of priests – their number equalling the king's age plus one – take turns praying. On the second day Muslim subjects visit the throne room. On the fourth day the king has a ritual bath. On the fifth day the royal family must take an oath of loyalty to its people.

WORDS TO KNOW

Altar: A table on which worshippers leave offerings, burn incense, or perform ceremonies.

Buddhism: A religion based on the teachings of Gautama Buddha, who lived in India in the fifth century B.C.

Civil war: A war between citizens of the same country.

Colony: A land that is ruled by people from another country.

Deity: A god or goddess.

Delta: The area near the mouth of a river that divides into many smaller streams on its way out to the sea. The land that lies between these streams is rich and fertile.

Enlightenment: In Buddhism, the attainment of a state of supreme spiritual wisdom known as *nirvana*.

Hinduism: The main religion of India. Hindus worship many deities and believe that a person's soul is born again, after death, into another body.

Immortality: Living forever.

Incense: A mixture of gum and spice, often shaped into thin sticks or cones, that gives off a pleasant smell when burned.

Lunar calendar: In this calendar a month is the time between two new moons — about 29 days. Many Cambodian holidays are based on this calendar.

Meditate: To sit quietly and concentrate on something, whether an idea, an object, or oneself. Meditation is an essential part of Buddhism.

Muslim: A follower of the religion of Islam.

Monk: A man who devotes his life to his religion and lives in a monastery.

Pagoda: A tower, usually built as part of a temple, with upward-curving roofs.

Solar calendar: In this calendar the months are 30 or 31 days long and follow the movement of the sun.

Temple: A place of worship.

ACKNOWLEDGMENTS

WITH THANKS TO:
Collection of Sayron Lao.
Vale Antiques, London.

PHOTOGRAPHY:
All photographs by Bruce Mackie except: Marshall Cavendish pp. 10, 14, 19. John Elliott pp. 11, 15.
Cover photograph by Corbis/Kevin R. Morris.

ILLUSTRATIONS BY:
Fiona Saunders pp. 4 – 5. Tracy Rich p. 7. Maps by John Woolford.

Recipes: Ellen Dupont.

SET CONTENTS